MW00579465

When Did I Become the Dumpster?

Raising & Teaching Rebellious Teenagers

By Joanne Colombini

Copyright © 2023 Joanne Colombini. All rights reserved.

No part of this book may be reproduced or transmitted in any form or by any means, graphic, electronic, or mechanical, including photocopying recording, or taping without the written consent of the author or publisher.

Briley & Baxter Publications | Plymouth, Massachusetts

ISBN: 978-1-954819-91-7

Book Design: Stacy Padula

To Almighty Father who gave me the skills and talents to write this book.

To Jesus Christ who gave me His words to write this book as an easy-read.

To the Holy Spirit who gave me the energy and motivation to complete this book.

To my sons, Dom and Frank, gifts from God. I love you equally and endlessly with every beat of my heart.

Preface

When Did I Become the Dumpster? encompasses true, detailed stories to the best of my recollection about my experiences as a mom to Dom and a teacher of alternative high school students. One day while driving my car, I saw two dumpsters just sitting in an empty parking lot. I don't know how it came to me seeing them, but the title just did: *When Did I Become the Dumpster?* It just seemed apropos to my written stories.

Having no previous experience or formal training in the field of journalism, I was lost on how to write my book. Unhappy with the format, my first attempt was a disaster. For years the rough draft sat untouched in a file box. But what I start I finish. I set a goal by the end of Winter 2022 to rewrite *When Did I Become the Dumpster?*

Before I started a day of writing, I said one Our Father prayer, and thanked the Almighty Father, Jesus Christ, and the Holy Spirit. The second time around with heavenly intervention, the words just flowed and my book was written to completion.

Half of the proceeds from *When Did I Become the Dumpster?* will be donated to St. Lawrence the Martyr Parish Outreach and Food

Pantry in Sayville, New York; and the Lighthouse Missions, Bellport, New York equally. Both these organizations help the less fortunate children and adults of their community with the basic needs of life.

Chapters 1-6 Highlights

Dom was in middle school when these stories begin. The first twelve years of Dom's life, he couldn't have been a better son. It was his teenage years I could have done without. I use words like "brat" to describe Dom, but all is written in jest for this book. My firstborn has grown up to be a wonderful human being, successful in his own right, and a son I thank God was gifted to me. I couldn't be prouder of Dom.

Chapters 7-17 Highlights

The alternative high school students I taught were mostly juniors and seniors. My creative ideas and solutions you may view as humorous, non-traditional or "out of the box." During all my years in education, there was never a hair of doubt that being an educator of alternative students was my calling. I learned so much from them about life, caring, and really paying attention to the effects an adult can have on teenagers. I'm so grateful to each of them for being who they were, true to themselves.

All names have been changed except Dom, Dominic, Frank, Jane, and Meghan.

Chapter One
The Teenager Debut

"To an adolescent, there is nothing in the world more embarrassing than a parent." —Dave Barry

Where shall I begin? Dom was a smart, good-looking, confident kid who possessed a fun likable personality. But he thoroughly enjoyed pushing boundaries. I had no clue how I was going to cope as a newly single mom living on my own. Help me God! The teenager was ready for battle.

My son was an eighth grader and a member of his middle school's track team. One morning he got up for school, prepared himself so he'd be on time to catch the bus. Typical of moms on school days, I was in his bedroom to check on him when Dom decided to "up and rumble" at me. In translation, he should have checked his words. I can't remember exactly what he said, but I remember what I said to him.

I stood in his space. I looked up at my towering six-foot tall, stinking too big for his britches thirteen-year-old son. "You just disrespected me!" I said. "It is never ever okay to disrespect your parent; not now, not when I'm forty, not when I'm eighty, not when I'm dead! For that Dom, you're not going to track practice today." Track practice was a big deal to him because the team walked over to the neighboring high school and practiced with the high school track team. "Dom, when school ends come straight home. You look up the definition of "respect," write it down, and tell me how you disrespected me as your parent."

"I don't think so!" I couldn't believe he answered me back. The audacity of this kid!

"Okay Dom, I'll give you a choice. You can do what I said or go to track practice. If you go to practice, I will get in my car, drive over to the high school, park it, get out of my car, and walk onto the track field. In front of your coach and your peers, I will drag your ass home. Have a nice day."

I know you are wondering what this self-empowering teenager chose to do. Dom came home and did exactly what I requested of him.

Here is his apology note for your reading pleasure without the definition Dom copied to include the phonetic spelling of respect.

Dear Mom,

I think we or I should respect my mother because she is honorable, and she is my mother in a higher position than me. Therefore, consideration should be shown. Nobody deserves not to get respect. Respect is very important in life. If nobody gave respect than the world would be a disaster. War would be here. Nobody would like each other therefore they would fight. I don't want our relationship to be war. I want it to be good or very good.

Things that I do that disrespect you. I talk back to you. Talking back is a way of disrespect. Disrespect is bad, just like war is. I will try very hard not to talk back to you. I think a relationship is a two-way thing. I think sometimes you should loosen up too because I'm a teenager and that is my whole or part of my attitude. All things I say come out of anger. I don't really mean them. Believe me I will grow out of this stage. I don't know when but I will try very hard to. Please forgive me.

I love you,
Dom

I thought the note to be quite clever. Dom sure had a way with words. He managed to get the punishment completed and lectured me at the same time.

Chapter closed, I moved on to other tasks at hand. After the letter, all had been addressed and, in the past—for me, but not my son. Two days later, Dom was sitting in the front seat of my car while I was driving him to a friend's house.

"Mom, would you have done that?" he asked.

"Done what?"

"Would you have gone to the track field?"

"Remember this: what I say, I do."

Chapter Two
What Suits Me

"Conformity is the jailer of freedom and the enemy of growth." —John F. Kennedy

The story in the following paragraph was included to demonstrate that Dom's trendsetter mentality started early on in his life. I just didn't see it, yikes!

Winter was approaching and my little guy needed a coat. He was almost three when I placed him in the shopping cart and off we went to look at coats for boys. There was a brown coat, very stylish without a hood, and it fit Dom. I kept looking and found a green coat that met all my expectations. It had a flap over the zipper, a furry hood, and was long to keep Dom's body warm. I put the green coat in the shopping cart. With that, my son had a full-blown temper tantrum. His first ever! He wanted the brown coat. There was no way I was letting an almost three-year-old make that kind of decision. My "perfect" child continued screaming right through checkout.

Flash forward. Dom was sixteen years old and needed a suit. At the time, I didn't possess a lot of financial wiggle room to spend money freely. I decided on a good, reasonable place to buy him a suit, much to his disapproval. When we got in the car, I thought it was unusual that Dom let his younger brother, Frank, sit in the front seat. Soon, I would find out the motive for his deliberate "act of kindness."

We arrived at the destination. There was a parking space right in front of the store. Frank, Dom (I thought), and I got out of the car. We were almost at the store entrance when Frank tapped me on the shoulder to say mom you need to turn around.

Well, well, well! It seemed Dom was still in the back seat of the car with no intention of getting out. *Here we go again!* I thought.

I walked back to the car, opened the door, and looked at my son who clearly was not compromising on his "shopping standards" to try on suits in "that" store. The "uppity" brat was staying put under protest!

"Dom, I'll give you a choice. You can come with Frank and me into the store without an attitude so I can buy you a suit; or on Monday, I will take you to the bank. You can withdraw any amount of money you want from your bank account to spend on a suit, and I will take you anywhere you want to go."

He got out of the car. Unfortunately, there were no suits in the store that fit him properly. We left with Dom now seated in the front seat of the car wearing an "I told you so, mom" smile of satisfaction on his face. I was not happy.

No money was withdrawn from Dom's bank account but he got a top-of-the-line designer suit tailored, with shoes, a belt, shirt, socks, and tie.

How you ask? Aunt Jane, my son's Godmother who loves and spoils Dom, is a trendsetter herself. She totally gets Dom's need for his individual style.

All ends well. Dom looked so handsome in his suit. Thank you identical twin sister for coming to my rescue, being overly generous, and once again spoiling your Godchild.

Chapter Three
Behind The Closed Door

"There are two types of pain you will go through in life: the pain of discipline and the pain of regret. Discipline weighs ounces, while regret weighs tons." —Jim Rohn

Foolishly I thought things had settled down. After all, Dom was a mature high school senior. Common practice raising my son was to have a curfew based on his age. The first half of Dom's senior year, midnight was his curfew, and then I raised it to 1 a.m. after January 1st. This was a fair curfew in my eyes. It made perfect sense to me. The last movie in most theatres would start by 10 p.m. giving Dom plenty of time after the movie ended to eat with his friends and be home by his curfew. *Wrong!*

In Dom's true-to-self personality, he continued to push the boundaries. I stayed awake every time he went out until he was safely home. It was a smart thing for me to do as a mom, and it turned out to be quite informative. My self-empowered teenager kept walking in

1

the door, late at 1:03 a.m., 1:10 a.m., 1:25 a.m., etc. Dom thought nothing of disregarding his curfew as if it never existed.

Finally, I had had enough of his nonsense. "Dom, a one a.m. curfew means you are in the house and your rear end is behind the closed door by that time. Consider this your warning: If you choose to break curfew one more time, you will pack your bags and go live with your father."

Dom heard me but did he listen? No! What a brat! He followed up my warning by breaking his curfew and arriving home, late at 1:40 a.m. Unbelievable!

As a parent, what I say, I do. I knew it was time to once again put my words into action. I got out of my bed.

"Pack your bags; you are going to live with your father now."

No response, not even a dirty look. Instead, Dom called his father and totally ignored me. He was still being a brat only a disrespectful one! The next thing I saw was Dom in his father's truck parked in the driveway. Nothing was happening except the two of them talked for longer than I thought necessary.

I went outside, knocked on the passenger window, and informed Dom that when he was finished chit-chatting with his father to get upstairs and pack his bags. I went back to my bed to "watch" television. I was calm and collected while dealing with this nonsense.

About ten minutes later, Dom came upstairs and went straight to his bedroom. After a little time passed, he came into my bedroom to ask me if he could leave in the morning because he had laundry to do. I thought to myself, *creativity at its finest hour!*

"No, you are leaving now. Your father has a washer and dryer. You can do your stinking dirty laundry there."

The packing was finished and Dom was at the top of the stairs ready to leave.

I looked straight at my disobedient son thinking, I have two roles, your mom who never ever stops loving you no matter what you say or do; and your parent who right now doesn't like your behavior.

I'm sharing with you Dom's departing words.

"I just want you to know that I have lost most, if not all of my respect that I had for you. No kid should have to deal with this, and I will be scarred for the rest of my life. I would appreciate it if you would consider me as an acquaintance, and not your son anymore. Mom, believe me, it is gonna take a lot to get me back; and I'll make sure you don't see me for a long time. Good day."

In retrospect, I was laughing while typing his quote for my book. Dom had great communication skills. He knew exactly how to deliver his message.

I looked at my son still standing on the top stairs and holding on to the railing swaying a little, delaying his departure. He was clearly upset which made it so hard for me to resist changing my mind.

"You can return tomorrow if you respect me, and the rules of the house," I said to him. He left mad and in disbelief that what I say, I do.

After four days, Dom told his cousin Meghan how terrible it was not to be able to go home and sleep in his own bed.

Meghan is my twin sister's daughter. Dom and Meghan are more than cousins. Identical twins have the same genetic makeup, so Jane and I treat our kids as half brothers and sisters. I got the inside scoop from Jane about Dom. I knew it was just a matter of time before I heard from him.

It took my firstborn two weeks before he called me. He wanted to return home. I was happy we talked things over. I received a sincere apology. Dom agreed to call me if he was running late returning home so I didn't needlessly worry about him, with the understanding that did not mean every time he went out for the night he could return home past his curfew.

All was well! Happily, he slept in his own bed that night and thereafter until he left for college.

Only a fool would underestimate Dom's ability for pushing the boundaries. It wasn't over yet!

Chapter Four

A Sagittarian at Heart

"The truth is more important than the facts."—Frank Lloyd Wright

Woodstock '99! Chaos! Confessions! It all began when Dom asked me if he could go to Woodstock '99 for four days with about twenty or so of his friends and classmates. After all, he was eighteen years old and leaving for college the following month. How could I say no to a chance of a lifetime for him? Anyway, it could never be like the original Woodstock.

Networking and rules were put in place between all the parents and teenagers. All granted the final "stamp of approval."

My new car was the transportation for three of Dom's friends, and his cousin Meghan. My son was the designated driver. They were off! Our teenagers reached their checkpoints and called us, to all the parents' relief.

The news stations reported daily on Woodstock '99. Overall, the reports were positive with the exception of the high costs for food and drinks. All was going good with the kids each time they called us to check in. Four days later, they returned safely back home to Long Island. Thank you, God. It was over or so I thought!

After dropping off all his friends and Meghan home, Dom walked in the door. It was four o'clock in the morning. He was tired but pumped about his Woodstock '99 experience. He put his bag on the kitchen table and started to empty it. I sat down on a kitchen chair silently content that my precious son was safely home. Well, my contentment didn't last.

I became baffled as to how Dom could afford to buy the items he was placing on the table, quite neatly and with great care. "How much did all this cost you?"

"I didn't pay for it. I stole it."

I couldn't fathom why Dom thought stealing was okay. My son, a thief! Time passed, it's 5 a.m. and I was too tired to approach the subject.

"Goodnight Dom," I said. "Tomorrow when you get home from work, you and I are going to have a chit-chat upstairs."

I wracked my brain trying to think how I was going to punish Dom. I needed to send him a clear message that what he did was so wrong. I knew taking his truck away for a weekend would have no effect on him. An idea came to me; it was brilliant! A peaceful sleep awaited me.

Dom returned home from work the next day, and I asked him to come upstairs. He acted nonchalant about the whole thing. We were sitting in chairs that faced each other.

"I did teach you right from wrong …"

"Yes."

"Then why would you steal?"

Dom's rationale: the vendors charged ridiculous prices, which justified his stealing the stuff instead.

"It's too bad you didn't get caught," I said, "If I could track down the vendor, you would return the items, write an apology, and pay for everything. I know this to be impossible, so I took from you what you took from this unknown vendor. You will never see any of it again"—I donated the items to the Student Council where I worked in Nassau County to sell—"Dom, the only thing you can keep is the tee-shirt because you paid for it."

"You had no right to take my stuff!" He was furious!

"It wasn't your stuff because you didn't pay for it."

Dom stormed out of the house. I had addressed the error of his ways and it was a dead subject or so I thought!

The first semester of college was finished and Dom returned home. He threw his English notebook at me and said read this.

"It wasn't that long ago, maybe a month or so ago, that a conflict over values arose. It happened to be the day after my friends and I had come back from Woodstock. What happened was very serious, and it placed a large burden on my relationship with my mom. In the end though, it was a lesson learned.

At the Woodstock convention my friends and I were going to steal items from the vendors. Our reasoning was the over priced merchandise and food that they were selling was ridiculous, so we thought they owed us something.

Coming home to reality after a long, sleepless weekend was the best thing in aid of our recovering. On the contrary, coming home with stolen merchandise was not to my advantage. Sagittarians are supposed to be very honest, and I consider myself part of that belief. I was talking with my mom and it had come out of my mouth, intentionally I do not know, the way I had gotten all those goods.

Upset and very disappointed in her eldest son my mom put me through so much guilt. I had soon realized the audacity it took to make me behave like I had. Quickly, I had totally become regretful, and above all I have gained a lesson in values, and the importance of having them and the will to stick by them."

I thought it poignant to share with you, the reader.

I cried when I first read Dom's heartfelt essay and I cried once again typing it for *When Did I Become the Dumpster?* I was so proud of my son for recognizing and acknowledging the error of his ways while understanding the importance of values.

No worries from me, Dom was to become a fine upstanding adult.

Chapter Five
Free At Last

"Success is where preparation and opportunity meet."—Bobby Unser

The college of Dom's choice was far away. I referred to the distance as, "the other side of God's country." It was heartbreak for me to say goodbye to my son at the airport. He was growing up and heading into the next phase of his young life. New experiences and adventures awaited him as an Arizona State University (ASU) freshman.

It was my "good" fortune his dorm room was on the fifth floor with a window that was easily removable. Whenever Dom was in the mood to sit out on the ledge, he removed the window. His self-imposed rule: Only sit outside at night to avoid getting caught.

My son flew home on his first break. It was wonderful to hug him after missing him so much. He looked so healthy and happy to be home!

Dom told me about his dorm room, the window, and his nights hanging out on the ledge.

"What possessed you to think that removing the window was a good idea? You could fall and kill yourself. If you make the stupid choice to remove the window and another student is hanging out with you on the ledge, and falls off and dies, you'll be held liable. It's not smart Dom. Please don't do it anymore," I said.

"Okay! Okay! I heard you!"

Back at college the practice of sitting on the ledge continued. He hadn't listened to a word I said. That's my son, he knew better than me. After all, he was eighteen. Dom pushed his own boundary! In the daylight hours, none other than himself removed the window. Having enjoyed the fresh air and view, he put the window back in place and went to class.

Later there was a knock-on Dom's dorm room door. He opened it to find an ASU security guard standing there. "Please accompany me to the Dean's Office," the guard said with a stern look on his face.

The guard lived directly across from the dorm building where Dom was housed, knew it like the back of his hand, and went straight to the source of the "problem." Dom was beyond nervous!

An administrative reprimand ensued, and Dom was informed of a student who died falling off a ledge. When all was said and done, my son was threatened but escaped being expelled from ASU.

He sweated that one big time. The window was permanently secured and served its intended purpose—fresh air and light.

Freshman year was over and my eldest was home for summer. He earned high grades in all his classes and accumulated a year's worth of credits, but ASU was no longer the college he wanted to attend. It was a good college but located on the West Coast. Dom was ready to return to the East Coast.

"Don't worry mom, I already applied to the University of Maryland. I was accepted for the fall semester."

"How did you decide?"

"My friends and a few other people said it was a great college."

It didn't matter what I thought; his mind was made up without further discussion. With his girlfriend in tow, Dom drove to Maryland. They spent a half-hour touring the University and then off they went to Washington D.C. for the rest of the day to sightsee.

Another trip was made in July. This time Dom went alone to meet with a University of Maryland counselor.

"How did it go?" I asked.

"Good."

"Did you get a class schedule?"

"Yes."

He had enough of my two-question interrogation and off he went to be with his friends.

As a new incoming University of Maryland sophomore student, Dom was not afforded housing. All available rooms had been previously assigned; that was a problem for me. I tried every which way to locate a suitable place for my son to reside. After weeks of phone calls, I contracted and paid a non-refundable rent fee for a room in an on-campus fraternity house available for fall semester only.

It's the end of August. The University of Maryland was in sight. Upon arrival even though Dom and his father Dominic were tired, Dominic took his son all over the area to buy everything needed for the room and classes. At the end of a long day, it was finally time for Dom to unpack, settle into his new room, and explore his surroundings.

My phone rang and on the other end was Dom's father who was rightly upset. He had run out of his abundance of patience and needed my help.

"Joanne, he won't unpack. He doesn't want to stay. He doesn't like it."

"Put him on the phone," I replied and Dominic passed the phone to Dom. "Dom you can come home and enroll in Suffolk County Community College. You'll have a whole semester to figure out your next move." He happily agreed to my demands and was homeward-bound.

After many weeks of work, expenses and travel to get Dom set up for the University of Maryland only to come back home, a dirty little secret came out of his mouth.

"Mom, the counselor told me that the college might not be a good fit ..."

"Now you're telling me this?!" That was one of those times I just wanted to "kill" him.

The School of Visual Arts (SVA) in Manhattan, New York was next on what turned into another college venture. "Nothing ventured nothing gained" was one of my mother's favorite sayings. Dom did not need any encouragement in that area; it came naturally to him.

My firstborn was creatively gifted in many different ways. After a lengthy admissions process to include his art displayed and reviewed by faculty, he was accepted to start SVA spring semester.

I took a ride into Manhattan to help my son with concrete cinder blocks. It was an "honor" to do so. Most teenagers, Dom included, avoided doing anything with their parent(s). I should have declined the invitation when I found out what "the mission" was. The normal area where we needed to park was closed due to construction. We had no choice but to settle on a parking spot located streets away from our destination—the SVA student dorms. We each lugged two concrete cinder blocks in wheeled knapsacks through the streets of Manhattan around construction and up the elevator to Dom's dorm room. It took two arduous trips but the bed was now elevated with the concrete cinder blocks under each of four legs for more storage. Good idea, lots of work.

"Come on Dom one semester, that's it!" He wanted to major in film at New York University (NYU) Tisch School of the Arts. It was highly selective and admitted just 100 students in the fall semester only. Dom, thrilled to be admitted, started to look for an apartment with his father in New York City. He attended NYU Tisch School of the Arts his junior and senior years. He studied abroad in Prague and Cuba his last year before graduation. The latter offered my son another opportunity (say it out loud readers) "to break a boundary."

His project was a film centered on surfing in Cuba. There were restricted areas throughout the country. The Cuban surfers and Dom were prepared to surf when a different location with better surf was offered to him. A non-permitted restricted area for NYU students, he went anyway. It was an experience Dom wasn't going to miss, surfing with the native Cubans in good waves.

The professor/chaperone learned of his excursion. She was very upset. It was a serious infraction and could have jeopardized Dom's safety. As a penalty, his grade was lowered to a C+.

"I still passed mom!"

Dom was more than happy to leave his surfboard in Cuba for the natives to enjoy. It gave them a chance to surf with his kind of board.

With an NYU Tisch School of Arts degree in hand I was so proud of my son's accomplishments. I hoped the future was ready for Dom because he was definitely ready for it. I reflected on my job as an imperfect parent. My son had been prepared with the skills necessary to be successful in this world as an adult.

Could it be? Yes! Free at last, free at last!

Chapter Six
Judgment Day

"Be who you are and say what you feel, because those who mind don't matter and those who matter don't mind."—Dr. Seuss

It's over! Dom was a certified adult according to my definition. He earned a college degree, was gainfully employed full-time, living on his own, and paying his own bills. Dom earned the freedom to be in charge of his own life with all it encompassed. For me, I had my life back. It was a well-deserved break having "graduated" my child from teenager to adult. I survived, and he avoided being put up for temporary "adoption" (*never!*).

Jane and I were drinking coffee on a beautiful morning at her kitchen table when surprise! Dom came home unexpectedly for a visit with family and friends. He was so loved beyond words by both of us. We always looked forward to his conversations and tight hugs.

After a quick hello, Dom at 6'3" and twenty-four years old standing in the kitchen, turned towards me. "You were a 'terrible' mother," he said. "You insisted on meeting *all* my friends. I couldn't go to a party without you calling my friend's house to know whether the parents were going to be home. You gave me curfews. You were so strict."

Dom was dead serious and he meant it. The list of my terrible parenting was long. I sat in my chair, looked back at my successful adult son intensely listening to every word.

Without hesitation, I asked him to please write everything down, have his signature notarized, then bring it back to me so I could put his note in my file box. "Dom, when you have children, I will be happy to read your note back to you and discuss it."

I never received the notarized note. I wish I had gotten it for safekeeping. I never figured out why I was "attacked" out of left field by Dom, and I never bother to ask him. Maybe I will someday.

Parents have a history with their kids. It's all based on *their* memories, not yours. There are no "perfect" parents. It is always wise to acknowledge and apologize when necessary to your adult children for any mistakes you made while raising and/or "hurting" them. It's okay to share your wisdom and tell them what you wished you had done differently, if only you could change those mistakes in hindsight. A late apology is an apology just late!

Without hesitation, as an imperfect parent, I put into practice acknowledging and apologizing to my boys when they were adults.

To my twin sister Jane, thank you for sharing this wisdom. Now I pass it forward to you my readers, and this unrelated very short story for your entertainment.

Extra! Extra! Read All About It!

It was Christmas Eve 2021. Jane and I were sitting in her "Green Room" with Dom. He turns, looks at me, and says, "You know Mom, we don't agree on mostly everything."

"No kidding Dom." We laughed at the same time because it was something that had been understood for years. "Dom you know I love you no matter what."

"I love you, too."

What a blessed life God has given me with my firstborn son! It's my priceless gift to be his mom!

Chapter Seven
Would They

"It isn't where you came from. It's where you're going that counts."—Ella
Fitzgerald

I arrived at my destination on time, prepared to teach in one of the
three alternative high schools. The alternative high school
program consisted of teenagers that were drug users, violent
offenders, truants, and non-compliant teenagers who possessed a
broad-based knowledge of profanity and their in-school rights.

Before going to Room 220, I stopped by the office and asked
the principal that he not come into the classroom. I wasn't worried
about being on my own. I had good common sense and I was not afraid
of these students. He respected my wishes.

After leaving the office I walked a short distance and located
the room. I went inside and closed the door behind me. Approximately
twenty-five students were breaking pencils in half and shooting them
into the tiled ceiling. There was no semblance of order. I could only

describe the scene as "they" because the students were acting like untamed beings.

I hadn't yet introduced myself when four boys walked to the front of the classroom. They pushed over a four-drawer file cabinet. It was tall, full, and thank you God, locked. They waited for my reaction. While the four boys bounced their bodies, waved their hands in a "cool" manner, and directed inappropriate comments toward me, I walked over to the file cabinet dressed in my navy-blue skirted suit. Their language was obscene. They were enjoying the moment, very proud of themselves, and laughing up a storm.

"She thinks she's going to f---ing pick it up. She's f---ing too weak!" they said.

I ignored them. I was unaffected by their meaningless words. Neither being intimidated nor in shock at their behavior. I viewed this as my first test of many as their new teacher. I stood by the file cabinet and prepared myself to lift it up. It was about leverage and being a strong-enough female. I promptly picked it up. The looks on their faces were priceless!

"Boys you can take your seats now, thank you."

Alone for the first time with these students, in the front of the classroom I addressed the entire class. "My motto: I never surrender on you because you surrendered on yourselves, and I never surrender on my commitment to you. You don't have to like me. My job is to teach and your job is to learn. I don't care what you did yesterday. My business with you starts today. My name is Miss Colombini and welcome to my world."

I continued addressing the students, explaining the rules of the classroom: Respect, Common Courtesy, and Ownership. I gave them a handout describing each of these rules and the behaviors associated with them. I told the students that I too must adhere to the same set of rules. This was "our" classroom.

I walked over to the side chalkboard and wrote the words: "If you keep doing what you've always done, you'll keep getting what you always got." It was my hope that some if not all the students might take the time to read the "silent message" more than once and absorb it.

The class ended and I said goodnight to each of them as they left the classroom. I knew teaching in this alternative high school was going to be full of unique challenges and experiences for the students and me. I knew I would survive. The bigger question: Would they?

Chapter Eight

Death In The Classroom

"Never let the odds keep you from doing what you know in your heart you were meant to do."—H. Jackson Brown Jr.

In 1990, I used a tool called, "For Reality Of Your Dreams" (F.R.O.Y.D.). It was a yellow three-dimensional figure with a round stuffed body, pudgy rubber hands, and oversized black and white-laced shoes. His rubber face consisted of blue eyes, a dimpled grin, and a huge, rounded nose that hung to his chest. His clothes consisted of a yellow shirt with his name on it. The shirt had a thin black band around the waist and stood thirteen inches tall. F.R.O.Y.D. looked like a Martian.

It was 1999. Sorry to report, F.R.O.Y.D. died in the classroom. The boys of the F---- You (F.U.) Squad had decapitated him. The F.U. Squad was formed in honor of me! There were four members in the squad (all boys) who signed their names and F.U. Squad on their class assignments.

A teacher I worked with handed me F.R.O.Y.D.'s headless body and confirmed for me the F.U. Squad was the responsible party. My sadness did not linger. In this classroom, there was no such thing as an apology. This was not a group of students that you could talk to about respecting one another's property. They would just tell you to go f---- yourself.

I had to address what the F.U. Squad did to F.R.O.Y.D, but how? It came to me like a flash of lightning. *Why not!* I decided to have a funeral for F.R.O.Y.D. I dressed in an ankle-length black suit jacket with matching pants, a black shirt, and shoes. On the left lapel of my jacket was a red carnation.

Before class, I placed headless F.R.O.Y.D. in a shoebox and covered his body with black tissue paper. I used a small round table and covered it with a black tablecloth. I placed the shoebox on the table with a sign by his "coffin" that read F.R.O.Y.D. Included on the table were two boxes of munchkin donuts and a bud vase of flowers. On the classroom door, I posted a sign:

FUNERAL TODAY
F.R.O.Y.D.
DIED UNDER SUSPICION
PAY RESPECTS IN ROOM 220
BETWEEN THE HOURS OF 3PM- 6:30PM

The students entered the classroom. I was standing there very somber with their assignments in my left hand. The F.U. Squad came into the classroom. The reaction was just as I expected of them. "What the f--- is going on here. This is f---ing crazy!"

As the students approached me, I acted as if I had lost a sibling and spoke with deep sadness in my voice. I could have won an Academy Award!

"This is the way my culture mourns the death of loved ones," I said. "Please feel free to pay your respects to F.R.O.Y.D., have some munchkins, and here's today's assignment."

The psychologist came into the buzzing classroom to confirm what he was told by others. While shaking his head back and forth in disbelief, he looked at me. "In my twenty years of education, never have I seen anything like *this* before."

He stayed for a short while and then left still shaking his head. I found it humorous!

Message sent. Message received. My opposing reaction to the members of the F.U. Squad illustrated to their dismay, that I wouldn't surrender my commitment to them.

The class was over. I stood by the door to say goodnight to my students as they exited the classroom. This time it was most befitting to say, "see you tomorrow!"

Three weeks later, F.R.O.Y.D.'s head was found behind the bookshelf in my classroom. But it didn't matter anymore. With no emotional attachment, I threw his head in the trash.

Case closed.

Chapter Nine
Unexpected Company

"It is our choices, that show what we truly are, far more than our abilities."
—J.K. Rowling

I learned very quickly that there were many types of students labeled "alternative." As an educator, I thought it wise not to read the student files in advance of meeting each one of them individually. I believed my students should be treated with a clean slate, with no preconceived judgments based on someone else's interactions with them. My students were on equal ground with me. I never cared who your daddies or mommies were relative to school business, nepotism, or favoritism.

One of my students was a bit of a puzzle. Kevin was a quiet respectful teenager. I hadn't yet figured out why he was in the alternative high school but my communications with him gave me a huge clue. Kevin didn't "do" assignments. None period.

When he was enrolled in my class, it required him to complete work as part of his preparation to take and pass the related New York State (NYS) Regents Exam at the end of the school year. Kevin earned credits toward graduation if he passed both the class and exam. It didn't matter to him. It was just one more class to fail. I felt he was in a rut and had no clue how to get out of it.

When asked about his assignments, Kevin just smiled and told me with the deepest sincerity in his eyes and voice, "I did the assignments Miss Colombini but I left them home."

Every week the answer was the same. Kevin must have thought I had "stupid" on my forehead. My job was to teach and his job was to learn. He was in for the shock of his life! My plan was in place. In a non-threatening manner face to face, I asked Kevin for his assignments, to no avail. They were long overdue.

"Kevin, you can bring your assignments to school by Monday, or I will be happy to pick them up at your house on Wednesday." I said to him. He heard my words. Did he listen to them? No! Did he take me seriously? No!

Monday came and went, no assignments. I called his mom and confirmed my visit on Wednesday early afternoon.

The "Day of the Dawn" arrived and my plan went into action. I drove to Kevin's house and parked my car. After all, what I say, I do. I got out of the car and walked up the pathway to the front door. There I stood as my student came out of his house to catch the bus with nothing in his hands. It was perfect timing! The look on his face was of disbelief. He was in shock! A priceless reaction!

After a lovely visit and productive conversation with Kevin's mom, I left and drove to the alternative high school. As I arrived in the building, the principal called out my name. She couldn't wait to see me. With a chuckle in her voice, the principal told me of Kevin's reaction to my visit.

Still in shock Kevin had gone into the principal's office that afternoon. He choked on his words. "Miss Colombini showed up at my house!" he said.

The principal knew my plan; we had discussed it the previous week. "Miss Colombini told you she would be happy to pick up your assignments on Wednesday, didn't she?" Her response to him was nonchalant.

The charade was over. I knew he grew up a little that day. We forged a positive teacher-student relationship. Kevin agreed to be pulled out of a non-Regents class where he could be taught one on one in a small group, and complete his assignments in school. He mastered the curriculum, gained confidence, and learned testing skills.

I believe this old adage: you can lead a horse to water but you can't make it drink. I was proud of Kevin and Kevin was proud of himself. He took the opportunity afforded to him and made good choices moving forward. He passed the class and the related NYS Regents Exam with flying colors. Kevin felt successful! Good for him. There was hope in the air!

Chapter Ten

A Box Of Chocolates

"Do what you can, with what you have, where you are."—Teddy Roosevelt

This alternative high school encompassed a smaller enrollment capacity of students who typically did not "fit in" the traditional high school environment for individual reasons. In safe surroundings, they were free to be themselves without judgments from other students and the staff.

Some of my students had self-empowered privileged attitudes, others wore clothes that were covered with safety pins, some created "out of the box" looks, others were adorned in tattoos, and others stood alone. They were bright, inquisitive, and polite.

Frequently, I would start a lesson and be interrupted by students to explain why it was necessary and of value to learn what was being taught to them. It was just their personalities, which I didn't mind at all. They were aware that my class mandated a passing grade as well as the related NYS Regents Exam to earn credits toward graduation.

Before class started my students were given five minutes to settle in and enjoy figuring out the three rebus puzzles on the chalkboard. They were given five minutes before the end of class to pack up their possessions and chat. If they had any questions or wanted to speak with me this time was available for them.

One day, a quiet student named Michael approached my desk. The topic he brought up was a very unexpected one.

"Hi Michael, what can I do for you?" I asked him.

"I never get nineties."

"Michael, what's your favorite candy?"

"Ferrero Rochers," he answered.

"Michael, I will buy you the biggest box of Ferrero Rocher candy if you get a ninety percent grade or higher on the next open-book chapter review."

Michael was a bit surprised at my unusual answer so I repeated it to him. We shook hands to seal the deal. Class was over and Michael exited smiling.

I was not in the habit of using the term "test" because I myself was test phobic. Many students stressed out at the mention of the word. So open-book chapter reviews went in my grade book as test grades. I had to be politically correct after all!

It was my belief that students worked to their potential when there were challenges set before them. I had given Michael a new challenge. I was confident he was going to meet it. After work, I bought a huge gold box of Rocher candy. Two days later on a Friday, it was open-book chapter review "test" time. Class was over and "poor" Michael had to wait to find out if he met the challenge until after the weekend ended.

On Monday, each student was given his or her open-book chapter review "test" privately at my desk. The reviews were marked with the earned grade along with a brief conversation between us.

There was hustle and bustle in the classroom and Michael was next. He rushed up to my desk. He had earned a grade of ninety three percent on his open-book chapter review "test."

"You did it Michael!"

"I don't believe it! I don't believe it! I did it! I did it!" he said.

"Do you expect me to buy you Rocher candy every time you've earned a grade of ninety percent or above in the future?"

"Yes."

"Michael, you just proved to yourself that you are smart and capable of earning grades in the nineties. You won't need Rocher candy from me anymore."

I saw the wheels turning in his head processing what I had just said to him. Without further delay, I pulled out the huge gold box of Rocher candy and gave it to him. He earned it, deserved it, and had a right to have it all to himself. Michael was so happy about the Rocher candy and his grade in that order! He couldn't wait to go home.

He continued to earn ninety percent grades and above on more than one open-book chapter review "test." Michael felt smarter and his confidence improved over time. He passed the class and the related NYS Regents Exam.

Another student learned his potential and self-worth. Hope was still in the air!

Chapter Eleven

No, No Fight

"Life is ten percent what happens to you and ninety percent how you respond to it."—Charles Swindoll

This is a different kind of story about the same alternative high school and class that was discussed in the previous chapter. I had my own way of preparing students for their open-book chapter review "tests" every Friday. Because I liked learning to be fun, I came up with an idea and named it, "The Question and Answer Competition." My purpose for it was to give all students the opportunity to practice and enhance their abilities to retain knowledge of important facts covered in the week's current chapter and five general knowledge questions. For example: Who is the Secretary of State? How many Supreme Court Justices are there? Who is the President of the United States? What month/day is Flag Day? How do you spell Colombini? The students had no idea what questions I would ask and when during the competition. It kept them on their toes.

On Fridays I handed out their open-book chapter review "tests" along with the general knowledge questions on copy paper from the Question and Answer Competition the previous day. This was an opportunity for students to earn up to five points extra credit added to their "test" grades.

Frequently I made trips to stores near me and bought silly gifts for the winning team to make sure there was a readied supply of pens with feathers, pushback racing cars, oversized pencils, and anything else that students would love to show off. Also purchased were a variety of lollipops for all my students to enjoy before class ended.

It was Thursday once again, The Question and Answer Competition Day. The students were asked to push the tables to the back of the classroom. In the center of the classroom, I set up two chairs facing each other with a small table between them. On the table I placed a teacher's bell. The students lined up around the room. The first two brave souls were seated in the chairs and made condescending faces at each other. I explained the rules and asked if anyone had a question. The students knew what came next.

"Are you ready?!" I'd ask.

"Yes!"

"Are you sure?"

"Yes!"

For the first time, and only time, it was the boys against the girls. The boys hit the bell. The first question was won by the boys. The girls hit the bell. The second question was won by the girls. The boys hit the bell and the third question was won by the boys. It was unbelievable! The competition was going back and forth. With each question asked it became more and more competitive. The battle of the sexes ensued, the girls rooted for the girls, and the boys rooted for the boys. The students' voices had escalated from pure adrenaline. Who was going to win? It was almost over.

I was surprised when the classroom door opened and the principal looked straight at me. "I thought there was a fight in here!"

"No, no fight," I said. With a smile on my face, I impulsively added, "This is what I call enthusiastic learning!"

I apologized for the noise. The principal smiled and left the room. She was a great principal!

We finished the competition more quietly. The girls won.

Enthusiastic learning. Good answer Joanne!

Chapter Twelve
The Beat Goes On

"Those who dare to fail miserably can achieve greatly."—John F. Kennedy

I discovered when I taught in the alternative high school setting, it necessitated that I innately employ creative ideas, quick responses to situations, and to always be two steps ahead of the students. In lies the story of a student named Vinny.

In almost two years as a teacher working at this alternative high school, Vinny only once called me by my name. He never acknowledged me or responded to my common courtesy towards him. Good afternoon, Vinny I'd say. No response. Have a good day, still no response. I like your shirt Vinny, but no response. I did not exist in his world. You will soon find out why.

Vinny was street-smart, brazen, and one of my toughest students. He was well versed in the art of using a string of curse words, initiating class disruptions, and inappropriate behaviors. He was the leader of the F.U. Squad. The entire school year Vinny turned in his blank assignments with his name and the words F.U. Squad at the top of the page.

Vinny challenged all of my skills as his teacher. He was not receptive to learning responsibility, ownership, the class curriculum, accountability, and the beat goes on. His mindset seemed to be that the world revolved around him, and he was treated as such by other teachers. Unfortunately, Vinny had been elevated just below God. In other classes, he could walk in and out of the classrooms at will to hang out with the principal or roam the hallways, play poker for money, and do or say whatever he desired on any given day. Not in *my* classroom!

Every time a string of curse words came out of his mouth, I would go over to where he was seated and with deliberate intent, I'd stand right in his personal space.

"Vinny, profanity is not appropriate to use in a classroom or at a job. You can curse all you want in the street and most likely no one will say anything to you. Try not to use profanity in the classroom. Thank you," I said.

Over and over Vinny used a string of curse words to talk with his friends, and I would do the exact same actions and use the exact same words. In the beginning, it could be up to twenty times a class session, without exaggeration. Consistency was the key. After a while, it lessened because he didn't want to hear me anymore.

One day to my disbelief, Vinny started to read an extremely sexually graphic triple X-rated story he'd printed off a computer, out loud during class. It didn't bother him that there were females present in the classroom. I walked over to where he was seated; stepped in his personal space. "Stop reading that immediately!"

He continued to read ignoring my request. I knew the sexual harassment laws in my state because I was a certified N.Y. State Diversified Occupational Cooperative Teacher/Coordinator

(D.O.C.T.C.). I promptly informed the entire class of what they were aloud.

"Vinny, I could press charges of sexual harassment against you. Any student in this classroom has the same option."

He stopped, folded the paper, and put it in his pocket. When asked for it, he refused to give it to me. Without resistance Vinny gave it to the school psychologist.

I could not ignore this incident. It was documented on record. I decided to contact his mother. They were an Italian family. My mom and dad were both of Italian heritage. All my life was filled with interactions between my parents, grandparents, and myself. I felt confident handling this "tough" phone call.

Vinny was there when my call was made to his home. I introduced myself and told his mother everything that had taken place in class.

"Vinny you know Papa's dying?!" his mother said with passion in her voice. I visualized my Grandma Colombini, an Italian female in dark clothes, a little chunky in size, short in stature, beating her chest with her fist using that same passionate tone.

"Momma, she's lying!" he replied. "She's lying I swear!"

"Mrs. B., I don't lie or set students up," I said to her. "I love teaching and Vinny absolutely read this story out loud in class. Any student that was present could charge him with sexual harassment. If you like, I can make an appointment for you and Vinny to come to school. We could meet together to discuss all this in person."

"No, that won't be necessary, thank you."

I asked Vinny's mother, "Should I have any concerns about my safety?"

"Absolutely not Miss Colombini." The call ended.

Weeks later I met Vinny's mother at an open school night event. Was I wrong the way I humorously stereotyped her as an Italian woman! She was a beautiful young-looking woman fashionably dressed and so very nice. I liked her very much. We had a general parent-teacher conversation and neither of us broached the incident. It had been sealed in cement.

In June, toward the end of the school year, I was headed down a flight of stairs. I got to the school's first floor when I heard my name being yelled loudly and repeatedly by Vinny.

"Miss Colombini! Miss Colombini!"

I couldn't believe my eyes and ears. My instincts kicked in; I knew something was up. It was the first time in almost two years that I was acknowledged as existing in Vinny's world. He stopped on the staircase and looked straight at me. "Can you talk to my mom? She's on the phone."

"I'll come right now to speak with your mom," I replied to him. I went back upstairs to the office and without hesitation, I took the call.

"Mrs. B., I am truly sorry—as a parent myself—that you will not see your son graduate."

The call ended. The outcome: Vinny failed my class. Vinny needed my class to graduate high school. If he had completed assignments the last three terms, and he just needed to make up assignments for this term, I would have been more than happy to help him. But he had never done any assignments for me the entire school year. It was impossible for Vinny to be given a passing grade for my class. Also, he was required to take and pass the related NYS Regents Exam. I spoke with the principal and I declared Vinny an "unreachable" student. He viewed the alternative high school as his "playground." While Vinny attended the school, his mode of operation was always the same. I saw no growth in his maturity or any improvement in his attitude toward the benefits of being educated.

As his teacher who is an optimistic realist this was a heart-wrenching unsuccessful experience for me. I had to remind myself that Vinny's failure was Vinny's choice.

The school year ended. Vinny left school defeated. Sad but true.

Chapter Thirteen
Walk Of Life

"You will always pass failure on your way to success."—Mickey Rooney

Alternative high schools exist because of the need to continue the education of teenagers who lost the privilege of attending their regular assigned schools. The decision to send a student to an alternative high school was based on the individual student's record.

Tom was a quiet cooperative student. He had difficulty being his own person. He just followed along for the ride without the skills needed to take charge of his own life, to make good choices, and change behaviors that didn't work for him.

I was curious about this student. I believed he truly did not know what should matter to him or how to find the right direction. What Tom did know was to try hard to stay out of trouble long enough to be released from the alternative high school and be reinstated back to his home school.

With this brain of mine, I had to figure out a way to help improve Tom's lack of skills in making good choices. One day, how to do just that finally came to me.

"Tom, I need you to go into the hallway with me, please." He got up from his chair and met me outside the classroom. Once there, I asked him to look at the straight line made by the installed tiles on the floor. He looked at me as if I was crazy. That's a compliment for a teacher in an alternative high school.

"Tom, I named this lesson the "Walk of Life." I asked Tom to walk on the straight line only. He did pretty good. "The straight line represents how most people go through daily life, doing the expected things, following civil society's rules, sharing the sidewalks, following traffic laws, wearing clothes in public, etc. Left of the straight line is the choice we make sometimes to not be compliant and break rules. We have all been there and done that in our lives. Just keep in mind the straight line is the better choice. The right of the straight line represents an even better choice. You do something above and beyond that makes you feel good about yourself.

Do you understand the differences, Tom?"

He nodded his head yes.

"Okay, you're ready to begin your 'Walk of Life'." The hallway was long, perfect for this lesson. Tom walked along the straight line. I was to his right with my arm cupped around his arm. All of a sudden to his surprise, I walked him off the straight line deliberately. "Tom, you were left of the straight line. Did you make a bad choice, good choice, or an even better choice for yourself?

"A bad one, Miss Colombini."

"Can you give me an example of a bad choice you made this past week in school?"

Tom gave me a blank stare. He didn't want to tell me and that was okay. He knew what left of the straight line represented.

After a short while, Tom cooperated with some encouragement from me to talk and "play" along. He continued his "Walk of Life." This time, I walked Tom off the straight line to the right of the straight line.

"Did you make a bad choice, good choice, or an even better choice for yourself?" I asked again.

"An even better choice, Miss Colombini."

"Have you done something by choice that made you feel really good about yourself?" With a big smile I looked straight at him. "I'm giving you a break! That's a yes or no answer."

"No, no Miss Colombini."

"Tom, there is still hope for you yet!"

I walked him off the straight line a few more times. Each time Tom would respond with total understanding of his choices. I asked him to explain the straight line, so I knew concretely he comprehended everything.

"Here's a spreadsheet to keep track of your choices." I said, handing him a sheet of paper with a spreadsheet printed on it. "It doesn't matter what they were in detail. You just check off the appropriate column: Left of the Straight Line, The Straight Line, or Right of the Straight Line. I'm asking you to be honest with yourself. Please don't worry about completing the spreadsheet. There are no right or wrong answers or grades. Do you know why I want you to do this?"

"Yes," he replied, sheet in hand

"Why?"

"So, you know what I'm doing."

"It's not about me; I want you to see your choices on paper. The spreadsheet can stay in the classroom, and after one week, I'll take it and give you a new one. At the end of the month, we will total up the columns. This will help you know how much you are improving on making better choices for yourself. It's a life skill.

"I just need another minute and then you can go back to class." With deliberate intent, I slowly spoke these words to Tom: "Every second, of every minute, of every hour, of every day, I have a choice to change the direction of my life." I asked Tom to repeat what I said to himself three times. (This is a good method when you want to remember something.)

He didn't want to do it; but when I said it with him, it went okay. "You can go back inside now. Thank you, Tom. You did great. I hope you aren't tired after all that walking!"

Humor is good for the soul.

Chapter Fourteen

Men's Room

"In three words I can sum up everything I've learned about life: it goes on."—Robert Frost

As a teacher, I gave all students my trust upfront. If students lost it due to their own choices, it had to be earned back. That was not an easy feat.

Ricky was a likable senior who exuded charm. It was obvious that he was sabotaging his final year in regular high school. He was so talented, smart, and clear-thinking. He possessed good verbal skills and was very respectful.

Foolishly, Ricky thought that he could pull the wool over my eyes. He didn't. I knew exactly what he was doing every time he attended my class. Many times, I tried talking with him; but in his mind's eye, he wasn't ready to graduate. I think Ricky felt safe and comfortable in the high school environment. The future was unknown to him. That was scary for some students.

"Miss Colombini, I need to use the men's room," he said one day in class.

I promptly wrote out a pass that was very specific including time left, destination, classroom number, date, student's name, teacher's name, signature. Ricky was given the pass and with a bounce in each step he exited the room.

Approximately ten minutes later, he returned and sat down at his desk. Momma didn't raise no fool!

"Ricky, can you come here?" I asked and he did without hesitation. I got a confirmation on what I had seen from a distance. His cheeks were red and his hands were cold. "Do you see 'stupid' on my forehead? I know you left the building to smoke a cigarette." He just stood there and looked at me with sympathetic eyes. "Ricky, charm doesn't work on me. You made the choice to break my trust. It's going to take you a long time to earn it back."

Quick on his feet, he looked right at me and spoke his "words of wisdom" with a grinning face. "I have a right to use the men's room if I need to in the future, and you can't stop me."

"Ricky, you are absolutely correct that you have the right to use the men's room. Students are given four minutes between classes and a lunch hour to take care of their personal business. Don't think to ask me for any passes until you have earned my trust back."

Defeated, Ricky learned that what I say I do. The subject was addressed and closed. He earned my trust back. It took almost two months. The important part was his desire to do so.

I never knew if Ricky graduated or not. He was no longer in my class after the first half of the school year. I did see him one more time when there was a fight right outside my classroom. The two boys fighting kept banging on the classroom's outside door. I promptly went into the hallway and broke the fight up.

Flying up the stairs was Ricky. He came right up to me. "I heard you broke the fight up Miss Colombini."

"I did, now get back to class. Go!"

I wonder to myself sometimes what Ricky had done with his life. I think to a certain degree he charmed me! Oh no! Not good!

Chapter Fifteen

Mr. 180

"However difficult life may seem, there is always something you can do and succeed at. It matters that you don't just give up."—Stephen Hawking

I did not read student files. When I first met Adam, he was quiet, respectful, and seemingly harmless. In class he sat every day as a member of the F.U. Squad.

Another teacher in the alternative high school thought I should know about Adam for my own safety. He proceeded to inform me that Adam was a violent offender.

"Did you know Joanne, that Adam cut the throat of an old man to rob him, and he beat up his mom's boyfriend and threw him through the front window of their house?"

"No. I didn't know, thank you."

Whether it was true about Adam, frankly I did not care. I kept my first impressions of him; it was my way of avoiding predisposed prejudice against a student I needed time to get to know better.

There were necessary things to know about Adam to foster his success while attending the alternative high school, though. A judge mandated he attend anger management classes once a week, and that he obtains employment. If he did not comply with the judge's orders, at seventeen years of age, he was headed for hard time.

My responsibility as a D.O.C.T.C. was to find Adam gainful employment. I spoke with him about it. He did not want to be a cashier, deal with customers, or speak with anyone at work. Adam was willing to stock shelves in any store I chose for him. This was going to be tough for me because most retail employment consisted of front-end positions that embodied all of the things he didn't want to do.

I made appointments with different managers over several weeks, to no avail. When on the road headed back to the alternative high school, a store caught my eye. I decided to stop. Normally, I called to make an appointment first, but this one time I followed my instincts and took my chances that a manager would be available to speak with me about Adam. Standing at the front of the store observing the cashiers was a manager—and the right one. He had time to give me.

In our conversation, I explained that I was a work coordinator who was certified by NYS and that Adam—if he were hired—would be placed as a Cooperative Work Study student to earn school credits under my supervision. He would have monthly visits from me, and written evaluations based on our conversations and my observations. The manager liked the idea and was willing to hire Adam as a stock person only, starting at minimum wage. We agreed that he and Adam would meet Friday and that Adam would report to work the following Monday. I thanked the manager. Adam had a job offer!

Back at the alternative high school, my class was about to start. It was standard practice that the F.U. Squad sat together.

"Adam, I need you to talk with me in the hallway. I found a job for you," I said.

No surprise here, Adam just ignored me; he was with his "buddies." I walked over to the table where he was seated and stepped into his personal space. "I will give you five minutes to meet with me in the hallway or your name will be put at the bottom of my list for job searches."

No comment. He didn't even look at me.

This was going to be Adam's hardest decision to date: his loyalty to the F.U. Squad or himself. I knew it and he knew it.

Adam eventually met me in the hallway. This was a good first step toward a new direction in his life. I informed him about the stock job with all the details of being a Cooperative Work Study student, the hours he would be scheduled to work, pay, etc.

He didn't say thank you, but I said loud enough for him to hear, "Thank you, Miss Colombini!" He returned to class without a word.

Adam was now employed and doing a fine job stocking items for sale. At the first of my monthly evaluations and observations of Adam's job performance, I was surprised when he started a conversation with me.

"Miss Colombini, customers interrupt me to ask questions," he said.

"What do you do, Adam, when that happens to you?"

"I just find someone else to help them."

"That's a good solution, I'm happy to hear it." With a smile on my face, I looked right at him and said, "I hope you realize that's helping customers."

The manager was very pleased with the pace at which Adam worked and he had no issues to discuss with me. His monthly evaluations were satisfactory.

But boredom set in. Adam wanted to find a new job. He decided on his own to start looking for a different kind of employment.

Without my assistance, he secured a job collecting shopping carts at a supermarket. Was Adam starting to take charge of his life? Could I dream to think Adam was growing up a little bit?

Adam learned with my help how to end his current employment in the appropriate time and manner. He did exactly what I had taught him. The manager was sad to see him go but wished him the best. I discontinued his Cooperative Work Study student status in the previous store and opened up a new set of paperwork. The hours Adam had accumulated to earn school credits remained intact.

Soon it was time for my monthly evaluation and observation of Adam at his new job with the supermarket. While driving around looking for a parking spot, I noticed Adam sitting in the bitter cold on top of the carts he collected. He was wearing a hat and gloves but still looked uncomfortable. There wasn't one stranded shopping cart left anywhere. I knew Adam took his job seriously.

I got out of my car to speak with him. "How are you doing?"

"Okay."

"Are you cold?"

"No."

"I'm glad you had a hat and gloves to wear today."

"Miss Colombini, my manager bought the gloves for me."

Instantly it put a smile on my face. "That was really nice of him."

"I told him thank you."

I proceeded to go inside the supermarket to speak with the manager. Things were going smooth and I received a great report on Adam. As I was headed back to my car, I saw him once again. "Keep up the good work, Adam!"

"Bye, Miss Colombini," he said.

Adam did so well collecting the shopping carts outside the store that the manager decided to assign him to the dairy aisle. Amazing for a student who had anger management issues!

I placed several Cooperative Work Study students whose work was satisfactory, in job positions. Adam was my best student placement. He earned school credits, and grew in maturity and appropriate attitude. Adam never displayed his anger towards me or anyone else in school or on the job site. He was learning self-control. I decided he was to be my Cooperative Work Study Student of the Year.

I approached the principal and asked if I could present a plaque to Adam at the graduation ceremony. I also wanted to invite his father, the judge, his home district high school principal, and his previous and current employers.

"Yes, certainly Miss Colombini. That's a fine idea, the principal said about my graduation ceremony ideas for Adam

"I'm very excited to get started!" I said. I purchased a cumulative yearly plaque for students' names to be memorialized as the Cooperative Work Study Student of the Year. Adam was the first student listed on the plaque. It was to be hung in the alternative high school's office. A personalized plaque for him to take was purchased as well.

Adam's graduation ceremony went off perfectly without a hitch! The "special guests" who attended on Adam's behalf stood up one at a time during the ceremony and were introduced to the audience. Adam had no idea he was to receive an award until I presented him with the Cooperative Work Study Student of the Year plaque. This violent offender had turned his life around 180 degrees.

Every once and a while, Adam comes to mind and I hope he kept on going down the path of life that brought him only good results.

My life as a teacher was changed post Adam. I learned an invaluable lesson: Never give up. I kept faith in my heart that more alternative high school students would make the right choices necessary to better their lives, just like Mr. 180!

Chapter Sixteen
Front And Center

"It takes courage to grow up and become who you really are."—E.E. Cummings

In this story, Dan was one of the youngest students in the alternative high school, to my knowledge, and was immature for his age. He was charismatic, full of energy, likeable, and smart. He loved being the center of attention. He was not ready to be a Cooperative Work Study student.

Having no choice, I found a job for Dan in an established variety store. It was big, clean, well-organized, and the manager was "user-friendly." The job entailed customer service and stocking shelves; it did not require cashier duties.

Dan was hired to work as a Cooperative Work Study student under my supervision to earn school credits. I had my doubts about whether he would be successful or even last a week. He liked to smoke pot. I knew the likelihood he would be high at work was more than a 50/50 chance.

Dan was employed for one month and it was time for my first work coordinator's visit to his job site. The manager was thrilled with him. He was a hard worker. His co-workers and the customers loved him. I was relieved to hear it. He received a satisfactory evaluation towards earning school credits.

My next work coordinator's visit was one month later. The report on Dan was just the opposite. Unfortunately, he had decided to steal approximately $500 worth of goods in exchange for pot. I spoke with the manager, apologized, and fully intended on terminating the placement immediately. To my surprise, when I informed the manager of this decision, he said he felt strongly about Dan being given a second chance having been in jail for drugs himself. This well-intended manager thought he understood Dan enough to be his mentor.

"I am not happy," I said to Dan regarding the incident. "You have embarrassed the school, yourself, and me. The manager does not intend on pressing charges. Against my better judgment, you have been graced with a second chance. Dan, one more offense you're out."

"I know Miss Colombini," he replied.

I spoke with the manager later, and made sure he understood that if Dan did one more out-of-line thing, the placement would be terminated immediately. At my request, the manager agreed to my work coordinator's visits changing from once a month to once a week. I thanked him for taking the time to speak with me.

I left the store. I couldn't have left fast enough! It had taken Dan under two weeks before he'd attempted and got caught stealing for a second time. I received a call from the manager and met with him the same day. It was my priority that Dan exit the store and have the Cooperative Work Study placement terminated, effective immediately.

Upon exiting the variety store, Dan said goodbye. He never thanked or apologized to the manager. Dan was just being Dan.

Sadly, being fired and ending his employment was not an effective-enough consequence. The likeable employee who smiled most of the time shrugged off all of what had taken place. At that moment in time, it did not affect him in the least. His immaturity was front and center.

I believe Dan was eventually removed from the alternative high school because to the best of my recollection, I do not remember seeing him at school a week after he'd lost his job at the variety store. There was a better placement for him to come. I wholeheartedly agreed—rehab anyone?

Chapter Seventeen
Full Circle

"Setting an example is not the main means of influencing others—it is the only means."—Albert Einstein

My twin sister Jane and I decided to stop at the local diner for some coffee and eggs one year. We needed a break from shopping during the fast-paced Christmas season. The waitress seated Jane and me in the very last booth available in the back. Right across from us was a mixed group of six teenagers all around 17 or 18 years old. We thought for sure they were going to disrupt our quiet. They laughed, had fun teasing each other, and counted their pooled money before ordering their dinners. But for someone who had an abundance of experience with teenagers, I was pleasantly surprised when they behaved themselves, kept their voices to a reasonable level, and did not use curse words to talk. One of my favorite pleasures: catching kids doing good or the right thing.

After we finished our meal, I spoke with the waitress and paid the teenagers' bill and the tip.

While I was in the diner's ladies' room, the waitress told the teenagers their bill had been paid. When I returned to my table the teenagers were a bit puzzled, but thanked me wholeheartedly. They didn't get why I did that for them. They had looked over at my twin sister Jane after speaking with the waitress and asked, *Is she rich?*

"It's called 'a random act of kindness'," I said to them. "You all behaved so appropriately for your ages. I needed to do this for you. What I would like you all to do is pay it forward sometime. That means doing something nice for someone else. For example, take the garbage out for your mom, play with your younger brother or sister, clean your room; set the dinner table, etcetera. Or you can do something for a stranger. Offer help to an elderly person, open their car door, or just say hello, give a smile, etcetera." Satisfied they understood what I said, I wished them all a Merry Christmas and said, "Be proud of yourselves, you are really nice "kids!"

About one year later, I attended a fundraiser for a police officer who was battling cancer. As I was putting food on my dish, a girl tapped me on the shoulder.

"All night I've was trying to figure out why you looked familiar to me," she said. "You're the lady that paid for our dinners in the diner last winter!" She told me how she and the other teenagers left the diner and went to the mall. For over an hour, they opened doors for shoppers. "It was so much fun. We got so many thanks and Merry Christmas wishes. I'm so glad I met you."

"That makes me very happy that you all followed through on paying it forward," I replied. "I hope you all continue the practice for a lifetime, and maybe teach others what I taught you. It was so nice to see you again and to update me."

We hugged, said goodbye, and wished each other a Merry Christmas and a Happy New Year. I was personally thrilled that the "random act of kindness" with teenagers whom I never met before went full circle, and I was able to hear about it.

I learned a valuable lesson from the incident: Never underestimate any teenager's capacity to care, listen, and choose to step outside his/her self to do good for others.

Colombini-Isims

These are expressions and beliefs that I will continue to say until I can't remember them anymore!

A late apology is an apology just late

Charm doesn't work on me

Crystal clear vision

Do you see stupid on my forehead?

Elevated just below God

Equal Opportunity: What is expected of all

Every second of every minute of every hour of every day you have a choice to change the direction of your life

Fairness: Addressing the needs of an individual student on any given day

For everything there is a choice

I call those the incidental nothings of life

I earned it, deserve it, and have a right to have it

I won't surrender on my commitment to you

I won't surrender on you because you surrendered on yourselves

If you keep doing what you've always done, you'll keep getting what you always got

If you're going to quote me, quote me correctly.

Just because …

Life interferes with living life

Mamma didn't raise no fool

Mommy doesn't go to school, you do

My job is to teach and your job is to learn

Not every question requires a response

Privilege is earned not given

Retrain the brain

Silent Messages

Teenager ≠ Adult

Thank you for proving to me I'm not perfect

The "total" student

The world does not revolve around you. You have to learn to revolve around the world

Toughness is in the mind

What I expect of you, I expect of myself

What I say, I do

With deliberate intent

With respect and responsibility comes privilege

You can accept guilt or reject guilt

You earned it, deserve it, and have a right to have it

The End

It's official.
Why are you looking for more pages?
You finished my book.
I know it was a short-paged book.
I thank you for reading it.
Share it with someone else.
You can close the book now.
Goodbye! Stay safe! Peace out!

Respectfully,
Joanne Colombini

Printed in the USA
CPSIA information can be obtained
at www.ICGtesting.com
JSHW062114060823
46000JS00005BA/163